Frankenstein's Guests

A comedy

Martin Downing

Samuel French—London
New York-Toronto-Hollywood

FOR AMATEUR PRODUCTION ENQUIRIES

UNITED KINGDOM AND WORLD EXCLUDING NORTH AMERICA

plays@SamuelFrench-London.co.uk

020 7255 4302/01

Each title is subject to availability from Samuel French,

depending upon country of performance.

CHARACTERS

Baron Victor Frankenstein, a scientist
Baroness Elisabeth Frankenstein, his wife
Ygor, his assistant
Frau Lurker, his housekeeper
Harry Talbot, a werewolf
Countess Ilona Bathory, the Queen of Vampires
The Phantom of the Opera, the Terror of Paris
Isabel Channing, his protégée
Count Vlad Dracula, the King of Vampires

The action takes place in the Great Hall of Castle
Frankenstein, near Ingolstadt, Germany

SCENE 1 Shortly before 7 p.m.
SCENE 2 Shortly before midnight
SCENE 3 A few minutes later

CHARACTER DESCRIPTIONS

The Baron is about thirty-five years old, of clean-cut appearance and speaks forcefully. He is an extrovert and emotional daydreamer.
The Baroness is twenty-seven, very attractive, but diffident and outspoken. She also likes a drink.
Ygor can be played at any age. He is a hunchback, ugly and scruffy, and speaks and walks like Quasimodo.
Frau Lurker is about sixty-five and has a dour and menacing manner. She speaks with a harsh German accent and marches rather than walks.
Harry Talbot is a good looking, athletic American in his midtwenties. Obviously a loner, but he does his best to be sociable.
The Countess appears to be in her late thirties and is both attractive and stylishly dressed. Her manner is restrained but can be passionate. She speaks with a mid-European accent.
The Phantom is about forty, but it's hard to tell since his face is generally concealed by a mask. He's French and his mood varies from one of menace to that of the sad romantic.
Isabel Channing is an American in her early twenties. She is pretty, cheerful, but occasionally abrasive. Like most of the other characters she's a total extrovert.
Count Dracula appears to be in his mid-forties. He speaks with a Romanian accent and his appearance is suave yet sinister. He's almost always formidable in his manner.

NB. It's important to remember that the "nasty" characters should play their parts with the right degree of malevolence, to strike a good balance with the comic elements in this play. The pace throughout should be *fast*.

Costume, make-up and special effects suggestions area given on page 52. The BBC Sound Effects Library comprises a wide selection of sound effects on CD available from French's Theatre Bookshop (send for a free list giving full details).

Other plays by Martin Downing
published by Samuel French Ltd

Full Length
The House of Dracula
The House of Frankenstein!

One Act
The Demon
Out for the Count, or How Would You Like Your Stake?

For my wife, Eileen, and son, John, who mean the world to me;

and for my nieces and nephews:
Claire, Rebecca, Kate, Daniel, Peter and Phillip.

With lots of love.

.

FRANKENSTEIN'S GUESTS

Scene 1

The Great Hall at Castle Frankenstein. Shortly before 7 p.m.

It is a scene of candlelight and long shadows. Black tabs, hung with old heraldic banners and positioned at an angle to the wings, form the walls L and R and gaps between these form exits to other parts of the castle. One DL leads to the dining-room and the kitchen, another DR leads to the laboratory, and a gap UR leads to the main door. UL we can see the bottom steps of a flight of stairs which leads to the upper levels. The only real wall is that at the back of the stage, which simulates old stonework. A huge fireplace, surmounted by jars of biological specimens and the odd skull, forms the central feature, with a "stone" pillar on either side. Above it hangs the Frankenstein crest. At the back of the fireplace is a secret panel which grants an exit off. A large baronial chair stands CR, to the side of which is a low table supporting a vase of flowers and a hand-bell. Two other tables, each carrying a lit candelabra, stand next to the tabs L and R. Another table, supporting a sherry decanter and glasses, stands UR against the back wall. There is an old sofa with cushions CL and two library chairs stand DL and DR

This is the scene which greets the audience after suitably sinister music has been played and the CURTAIN rises. From off R come the sounds of electrical equipment humming and sparking, accompanied by bright flashes of blue and white light

Baron (*off, shouting*) Have you done it?

Ygor (*off, shouting*) Yes, Master!
Baron (*off*) Then hook up the electrodes and count to eight!
Ygor (*off*) One, two, four, six…
Baron (*off*) Blockhead! (*Hastily*) Three, five, seven, eight! Turn that wheel! Faster — faster!

The electrical noises reach a crescendo

(*Off, yelling*) Now — stand back!!

There is a tremendous flash off R

Ygor catapults on to the stage, spinning in circles before collapsing in a heap. Seconds later the Baron enters, obviously excited, holding a conical flask full of fluid

(*Ecstatic*) I've succeeded! See for yourself! Creatures that move — creatures that breathe — creatures that live!!

Ygor rises unsteadily and takes the flask as it's thrust at him. The Baron clasps his hands together in delight as Ygor stares into the flask, bemused

Ygor They're noodles, Master.
Baron (*sharply*) What?
Ygor (*glancing up*) You've just created Minestrone soup — with noodles.
Baron (*desperately*) Rubbish!
Ygor A lot of folks say that, but it's still pretty popular.

To the Baron's dismay he slurps a large mouthful of the flask's contents

Baron (*throwing his hands up*) Damn! I can't fool anyone anymore. (*Glaring at Ygor*) Not even a cretin.
Ygor (*sotto voce, grinning*) Or a crouton. (*Offering him the flask*) D'you want any of this?

Baron (*shuddering*) No thanks. I can't stand things bobbing against my lips.
Ygor (*mischievously*) As if they were alive, Master?
Baron Shut up!

Ygor grins and continues to slurp from the flask as we hear the sound of the main door opening and shutting. The Baron turns to look UR

The Baroness stomps in, decidedly wet and carrying a bag with bottles in it. They clink together as she moves down C

Baron Ah, hallo Elisabeth. Did you have a nice walk?

He stares at her bag with obvious suspicion. During the following Ygor peers into it

Baroness (*irritably*) Are you serious? Halfway back from the — (*an obvious lie*) butcher's — the heavens opened and I got soaked! Ygor ——

He hastily adopts an innocent posture

— has the sun ever shone in this part of the world?
Ygor (*puzzled*) The sun, Mistress?
Baroness (*turning to the Baron*) You see! (*Urgently*) I'm telling you, Victor, I can't bear another minute in this damp, dark, God-forsaken old dump! You've got to take me away. Now!

As she moves towards him the bottles in the bag clink together and she clutches them protectively

Baron (*frowning*) But darling — my *experiments* ...
Baroness (*sharply*) What experiments? You haven't done anything useful since we arrived.
Baron (*defensively*) I made a big bad *monster*, didn't I?
Baroness Briefly. Then he went to pieces.

Ygor (*to the Baroness*) 'Cos he didn't use cross-stitch.

The Baron glares at him

(*Hastily*) But he's created a lively Cup-A-Soup!
Baroness (*drily*) Whoopee-doo.

Ygor sniggers as the castle clock tolls once

Baron (*sharply*) Listen to me — both of you! We can't leave. Not
   yet. Some guests are about to arrive ——
Baroness ⎱
Ygor   ⎰ (*together; sceptically*) Guests?

There is a stunned silence

Baron (*oblivious*) — and for reasons of anonymity and safety they
   have to spend the night here.
Baroness They must be mad!
Baron (*awkwardly*) No — but they do have *other* problems, and
   they'd like my scientific advice.

Ygor and the Baroness burst out laughing

Enough of that! Elisabeth — I suggest you and I get changed.

The Baroness raises an eyebrow and starts heading for the stairs

Ygor can help Frau Lurker with the food.
Ygor It's already cooked.
Baron And the recipe —— ?
Ygor (*dubiously*) Pot-luck.
Baroness (*drily*) Yummy.

*She mounts the stairs and exits, the bag of bottles clinking as she
goes*

The Baron immediately turns to Ygor

Baron (*conspiratorially*) How many were in there?

Ygor counts three on his fingers and then looks up

Ygor *Five*, Master.
Baron (*both annoyed and worried*) Damn!

  He hurries after his wife and exits

Ygor grins

Ygor There'll be fun in the old schloss tonight!

He starts heading L, then halts as the castle doorbell jangles

  (*Excited*) The bells! The bells!

  He gallops out UR and we hear the main door opening

Ygor (*off*) Y-e-s-s?
Talbot (*off*) I've come to see Baron von Frankenstein. Hope I've got the right place?
Ygor (*off; cod American*) You sure have! Come on in.
Talbot (*off*) Thanks.

We hear the door close

  Then Talbot steps into the hall UR wearing hiking gear and carrying a rucksack. He stares round the room wide-eyed as Ygor follows him in

Ygor (*over Talbot's shoulder*) You must be — (*ducking under his arm to look at the rucksack label*) — Mr Talbot.
Talbot (*turning to him*) That's right. You know me?

Ygor Not exactly — but your *fist* rings a bell. Heh, heh, heh!

He exits up the stairs, chuckling madly

Talbot *(drily)* Wise-guy.

Talbot goes to put his rucksack on the sofa

Frau Lurker marches in DL, holding a blood-stained meat cleaver. She stops short when she sees him

Frau Lurker *(fiercely)* Who are you?
Talbot *(eyeing the cleaver warily)* The name's Harry Talbot. And you're ——?
Frau Lurker Never mind! *(Eyes narrowed)* Why are you here?
Talbot *(nonplussed)* I'm a guest, ma'am.
Frau Lurker *(hissing)* You are a fool!
Talbot Hey?.
Frau Lurker *(advancing and gripping his arm)* This castle is evil! *Evil!*
Talbot *(wincing under her grip)* Oh yeah?
Frau Lurker *(grimly)* A young man, handsome und sexy like you, stayed here a year ago. Und in the night — *(she shudders)* — Oh! such terrible *screams!* *(Darkly)* Next morning we found him out on the drive — his clothes drenched in blood. But his *face* — *(Wide-eyed)* — *Gott in Himmel*, I cannot describe it!
Talbot How come?
Frau Lurker *(waving the cleaver maniacally)* Something had run off with his head!

Releasing his arm and cackling madly she turns and marches out DL as Ygor bounds down the stairs

Ygor *(gesturing)* The Master!

The Baron comes downstairs buttoning his dinner jacket

He extends a hand to Talbot, who shakes it

Baron Welcome to Castle Frankenstein, Mr Talbot. You had a
  pleasant journey?

*He gestures to Ygor to pour two glasses of sherry and he heads for
the table* UR

Talbot (*hesitant*) I guess so. Yeah. (*Darkly*) The thing is — I've a
  lot on my mind.
Baron (*nodding*) Indeed. And I hope I'm able to help you.

*Talbot and the Baron both sit, after which the Baron takes a letter
from his pocket and glances briefly at its contents*

Baron According to your letter; you're ... not like *other* men.

*Ygor, about to hand them sherry, takes a step backwards, wide-
eyed, before proceeding*

  Something which stems from a misguided stroll in the backwoods
  of Bavaria, where you — (*reading and grimacing*) — got bit real
  bad by a bad-tempered wolf.
Talbot (*grimly*) Yeah. (*He rubs his left thigh*) Right here!
Baron (*still reading*) And now, whenever there's a full moon, you
  become voraciously hungry — *hairy* ——
Talbot Sprout a mean pair of fangs ...
Baron (*grimacing again*) Your "pinkies" turn into claws ...
Talbot (*growling*) An' somethin' *humungous* busts outta my
  pants!
Ygor (*recoiling, hands over his groin*) Yerk!
Talbot (*emphatically*) Butt-side.
Baron (*impassively*) Where else?

*There is a pause as the Baron returns the letter to his pocket and
Talbot unconsciously scratches his rear. Then both Ygor and the
Baron burst out laughing*

Talbot (*sharply*) What's so funny?
Baron (*wiping his eyes*) Oh nothing — nothing ... (*To Ygor*) It's
a gem! *Priceless!*
Ygor A real *howler*, Master!

There is more falling about and Talbot jumps to his feet

Talbot (*angrily*) If this is the way you're gonna treat me, I'm
leavin'!
Baron (*recovering*) I'm sorry, Mr Talbot. We don't mean to be
heartless. It's just that ...

He giggles again

Talbot (*snarling savagely*) It's no joke!
Baron (*sobering*) No, no — I'm sure it isn't. But tell me — when
you're running around like a rabid Rottweiler, are you still Harry
Talbot *inside?*
Talbot Sure — but I can't stop myself from doin' — you know —
doggy things. Like chasin' cats, sniffin' trees an' — (*grimly*)
makin' a meal of anythin' meaty. (*Urgently*) I try — but I can't.

He falls to his knees next to the Baron

It's a goddamn nightmare, believe me!
Baron (*patting his head*) I do, boy...

He hastily withdraws his hand as Talbot tries to nip it

And I'll do my best to find you an antidote.
Talbot (*rising to his feet urgently*) But how soon? I mean, there's
a full moon tonight, an' it's a dead cert ... !

The Baron also rises

Baron (*cheerfully*) I'll start work in a jiffy. In the meantime, why
don't you unpack and relax?

Talbot (*knocking back his drink*) OK.

Ygor gestures to the stairs as Talbot picks up his rucksack

Ygor This way, sir.

They both start to move

It's one of the bigger kennels.
Baron (*sharply*) Ygor! The *Dr Pavlov* Suite.
Ygor (*grinning*) Sorry, Master.

Ygor and Talbot start to climb the stairs

As they do they meet the Baroness descending. She's wearing an evening dress with jewellery and holds a half-empty gin bottle and a glass which is half-full

Baroness (*eyeing Talbot admiringly*) Well, hallo.
Talbot (*nonplussed*) Hi.

He and Ygor exit

The Baroness saunters down to her husband, sipping her drink

Baroness Was that the first of your guests, Victor?
Baron (*frowning*) Yes, dear. A young American.
Baroness (*glancing at the stairs*) Quite hunky, from what I've glimpsed. (*Turning back to him*) D'you think he's a wolf?
Baron (*drily*) Not at the moment.

The Baroness, clearly disappointed, starts heading towards the exit DL, and as she does the Baron quickly removes the bottle from her outstretched hand. She makes a face at him

Baron (*pointedly*) Where have you hidden the others, Elisabeth?

She ignores him until she's just at the exit, then turns, tapping her nose and smiling. Following which she exits

Baron (*clearly annoyed*) Elisabeth — !

He marches out after her with a grim expression. A second later the doorbell jangles and Ygor bounds downstairs, excited

Ygor The bells! The bells!

The bell jangles again as he crosses to UR

(*Irritably*) Keep your knickers on!

He disappears off UR *and we hear the sound of the door being opened*

(*Off*) Wel-come to Castle Frankenstein!

We hear the door closing

Then the Countess Bathory glides in, closely followed by Ygor, who stares at her appreciatively

Countess (*gazing about her*) Good! I wasn't sure this was the correct destination.

Frau Lurker suddenly appears DL, *brandishing a meat skewer*

Frau Lurker (*fiercely*) It isn't! Leave *now*, while you still have the chance!
Countess I beg your pardon?
Frau Lurker (*grimly*) There was a woman — attractive, und sickeningly stylish like you — who stayed here a month ago. (*She shudders*) Und in the night ...
Countess You heard terrible screams?
Ygor (*shaking his head*) We heard nothing.

Frau Lurker (*irritably*) But in the *morning* ——

Countess She was dead and dismembered?

Frau Lurker (*folding her arms angrily*) Who is doing the frightening? Me or you?!

Countess (*startled*) You.

Frau Lurker Gut! (*Resuming her former manner*) In the morning we could not find a trace of her. She had *vanished*!

Ygor (*blithely*) With half the silver.

Frau Lurker (*furious*) Dummkopf! (*Clouting him*) You have ruined my story!

Ygor Ow! Sorry! *Ow!*

She grabs him by the scruff of his neck and marches him to the exit
DL

The Baron enters, calling over his shoulder

Baron I'll find them if it takes me all night!!

Ygor (*half-strangled*) The Master...

Frau Lurker drags Ygor out

The Baron approaches the Countess with a charming smile. She extends her hand to him

Baron Countess Bathory? (*Kissing it*) I'm delighted to have you as my guest.

Countess And I'm delighted to be here, dear Baron.

Baron Would you like a sherry?

Countess Thank you.

She sits on the sofa as the Baron moves UR *to do the honours, retrieving his own glass from the table* C. *He fills this, too*

Baron D'you know a Mr Talbot?

Countess I've heard his name mentioned —— usually in conjunction with a snigger.

The Baron smirks

It's said he's a bit of an animal.
Baron At times — and it's a strange tale.
Countess (*drily*) A bushy one, too.
Baron Er — quite. He's also my guest tonight.

The Baron approaches her and hands her a glass of sherry, then goes to sit in the baronial chair with his own

Countess I'm intrigued. Like me, he has come to seek your advice?
Baron Yes — but the two problems are very different. He's a werewolf.
Countess Whereas *I*, dear Baron, am a vampire!
Baron (*enigmatically*) Mmmm.
Countess (*sipping her sherry*) But we share one area of common ground, Mr Talbot and I: the night! The scene of our strange and unfortunate existence. (*Bitterly*) While all humans rest, we roam the darkened streets like characters in a macabre puppet show, dancing to the tune of their heartbeats.
Baron (*bemused*) But you have friends, surely?
Countess Friends?
Baron Other *vampires*.

He knocks back his sherry

Countess (*shuddering*) Such *bores*, dear Baron. Their only topic of conversation is the merit of one blood group over another! (*Bitterly*) And the zombies! Have you ever met one?
Baron I've *taught* a few!
Countess I mean the real zombies — victims of the Filofax cult who inhabit the restaurants of the inner cities, clutching their mobile phones, who exhort me and my kind to buy timeshare and drink gallons of mineral water! They're a real *joy*!
Baron So what d'you want me to do?
Countess (*urgently*) Help me escape this hellish existence before further exposure to the tribe of the Living Dead makes me totally and unutterably morbid! (*Pleading*) D'you understand?

Baron (*rising*) Indeed. And I'll do all I can to help you.

He rings the handbell as the Countess also rises

Countess (*fervently*) Thank you.

Ygor gallops in from DL.

Ygor (*excited*) The bells! The ——
Baron (*sternly*) Ygor!
Ygor (*abashed*) Sorry, Master.
Baron Show the Countess to the Lugosi Suite.
Ygor (*saluting grotesquely*) Yes sir!
Countess And there's five pounds if you transport my luggage from the doorstep.
Ygor (*grinning*) *Fangs!*

The Baron raises his eyes as Ygor escorts the Countess upstairs. The Baron goes to look after them

The Baroness saunters in DL, *now holding a different glass and with one hand behind her back. She glances at the Countess as she and Ygor disappears from view*

Baroness And who might *she* be?
Baron (*without turning*) The Countess Bathory.
Baroness (*unimpressed*) Really?

She moves to the sofa and quickly puts the gin bottle she's been hiding behind one of the cushions. The Baron turns with a mischievous smile

Baron Rather luscious — from what I've *ogled*.
Baroness (*sharply*) I'd say she was a vamp!
Baron (*rubbing his hands*) Definitely.
Baroness (*angrily*) Oh, Victor!

She turns and exits haughtily DL. The Baron goes straight to the sofa and finds the bottle, which he pockets with a smug grin. Then he follows her out. A second later we hear the main door bang open and then Isabel Channing rushes into the hall UR clutching a small suitcase and pursued by the grim figure of the Phantom of the Opera. He is doing his best to catch her, but she eludes him by running round the furniture

Isabel Keep your filthy murderin' hands *off* of me!

Phantom Not until you 'ave 'eard what I 'ave to say, ma petite! (*Lunging at her*) I took you from nowhere ...

Isabel (*dodging him; incredulous*) Are you kiddin'? I'd a solo spot at the *Moulin Rouge*!

Phantom Tried to make you sing ...

Isabel What a hoot!

Phantom (*angrily*) And this is 'ow you *thank* me — by 'iding with strangers!

He manages to catch her by the arm. She struggles to escape

Isabel Let me go — *freako*!

Phantom (*suddenly gentle*) Isabel ... *Chérie* ...

Isabel Don't you dare sweet-talk me, you louse!

Phantom Say you'll be my love forever ...

Isabel (*wide-eyed*) Oh no!

Phantom Say we'll live as one, together ...

Isabel I'm gonna puke!

Phantom Say the words and I will be your *slave.*

Isabel (*yelling*) Help!!

She pulls herself free and immediately bats him in the groin with her suitcase

She rushes off upstairs

Phantom (*doubled up*) Ugh!

*He hurries towards the fireplace, still in great pain, and takes a
letter from his pocket which he drops on the floor. He then
disappears into the fireplace. As he does, the Baron, Frau Lurker,
Ygor and the Baroness (still holding her glass) rush in* DL

Baroness (*peering round*) Who screamed?

*The Baron crosses the hall, frowning, and then notices the letter on
the floor. He stoops to pick it up*

Baron (*bewildered*) The postman by the looks of it.
Baroness (*reaching for the letter*) What's he brought?
Frau Lurker (*grabbing at it too*) I'll see.
Ygor (*ditto*) No — *me!*
Baron (*snatching it away from them*) Please — it's not a Pools win!

The others listen avidly as he reads aloud

"Baron, I am sending you a note of the most malevolent nature. Pay
close attention if you value your life." (*Wide-eyed*) What the ... !

*Organ music is heard as the Phantom's voice takes over and
everyone stares above and around them, bewildered*

Phantom (*off*) That delight of the Paris stage, Mam'selle Channing
'as entered your château and I am anxious you do not meddle with
'er singing career. Be prepared for something *nasty* should you try
to interfere!

The voice and music fade out

Baroness (*bewildered*) Who on earth's sent this?
Frau Lurker (*pointing to the signature*) P.O.O.
Baron Who the hell's that?
The Others *Poo!*
Baron (*drily*) That's really not amusing.
Frau Lurker (*pointing to Ygor*) He said it.

Ygor No, I didn't!
Baroness Yes, you did!

There is a sudden pounding on the main door

Baron *Quiet*, all of you!

The pounding is repeated and the Baroness knocks back her drink desperately

Baroness I'm off!

   She exits at top speed DL

Baron (*calling after her*) Don't be idiotic!

The pounding occurs again and he looks nervous

   Answer the door, Ygor, while I put this somewhere safe ...

   Waving the letter he races off after his wife

Ygor moves towards the exit UR

Ygor (*scared*) If I die before I sleep, I pray the Lord my soul to keep!

   He disappears and we hear the sound of the door opening

   (*Off, timidly*) Welcome to Castle... *Yikes*!

   He gallops back in, terrified, with Count Dracula on his heels. He strides DR *looking totally sinister*

Count (*deadly*) Good-evening.
Frau Lurker (*wide-eyed*) Mein Gott!
Count I'm here to see your master, the Baron.
Frau Lurker (*bravely*) He isn't here. *No-one* is here. This house is cursed — CURSED!

Count Really?

Frau Lurker Ja! There was a man — tall und dark like you, only he wasn't so *pale* — who stayed here to finish a poem.

Ygor (*hastily*) A week ago.

Frau Lurker But he never had the chance. (*Wide-eyed*) When I went to take him cocoa — (*She shudders*) Something had made him eat his own words!

Count (*shrugging*) It sounds like poetic justice.

Frau Lurker (*fiercely*) It's *proof*, mein Herr. Proof that no-one leaves Castle Frankenstein alive!

Count (*grimly*) Well I'm already *dead*!

Ygor
} (*together, wide-eyed*) Eh?
Frau Lurker

Count (*sharply*) So cut the Gruesome Twosome act and clear off! *Now*!

Ygor (*terrified*) Yes sir!

Frau Lurker (*ditto*) At once, mein Herr!

They both rush towards the exit DL.

As they're about to exit Ygor and Frau Lurker collide with the Baron, who's entering. He holds another bottle of gin which he's passing from hand to hand, looking pleased with himself

Ygor (*over his shoulder*) The Master!

Frau Lurker Gott help him!

They exit

The Baron sees the Count and pockets the bottle hastily

Count Good-evening, Herr Baron.

Baron (*warily*) Good-evening. You must be —— ?

Count Count Dracula.

Baron (*choking*) *Dracula*?

Count (*irritably*) That's what I said — and I've come here, albeit unexpectedly, to consult you on a personal matter.

Baron So long as that's *all*.

Count Don't wet yourself. I've already snatched a quick bite.

Baron (*alarmed*) *Here*?

Count (*shaking his head*) In the village. The local equivalent of haggis. (*He rubs his stomach, grimacing*)

Baron You should have had the steak ...

The Count glares at him

But — how can I help you? (*He moves to sit*)

Count (*pacing the hall; grimly*) My problem concerns your previous guest the Countess Bathory.

Baron Oh yes?

Count Ilona and I have known each other for many years — centuries, in fact — and in eighteen forty-four we became engaged.

Baron (*tentatively*) A hasty decision?

Count Far from it. We were mature in outlook and marriage seemed logical.

Baron (*quizzically*) Before or after the millenium?

Count We'd not fixed a date. (*Sadly*) And it seems we never shall. Ilona's changed her mind.

Baron (*faintly*) Oh dear.

Count (*with increasing passion*) Because she's bored with our decadent lifestyle — bored with the one-night-stands — bored with the dismal company of our kind... (*With real anger*) Bored, in fact, with *me*! Count Vlad Dracula! A prince of the Magyar race! How's this *possible*?!

Baron (*stifling a yawn*) It's hard to say.

Count (*grimly*) It wasn't for *her*! "Life with you sucks!" "Flit off!" (*Desperately*) What am I to *do*?

Baron Forget you ever met?

Count I can't! Like a magnet, she still draws me wherever she goes. That's why I'm here tonight. (*Weakly*) But to win her back I must change, which seems impossible — apart from becoming a bat — and to leave her would be torment! That, too, is impossible. (*Desperately*) *I* can't reconcile such impossibilities. Can *you*?

Baron (*hesitantly*) I'm not sure.

The Count scowls

But I *think* so. (*He rings the handbell hastily*)
Count If you succeed, Herr Baron, you'll earn my everlasting
gratitude.

Baron (*sotto voce*) A few quid wouldn't go amiss.

Ygor gallops in from DL.

Ygor (*excited*) The bells! The b-b-b ——

He stops short, seeing the Count

Baron Would you like B and B too, Count?
Count (*assenting*) If someone transports the long box from my
carriage ...
Baron (*wryly*) Certainly. Ygor — show the Count to the Crypt ...
Suite and then attend to his — his ...
Ygor *Coffin*, master?
Baron (*hastily*) Yes, well, *do* it!
Ygor (*to the Count*) I got a fiver for humping the last one. What's
yours worth?
Count (*grinning*) A bedtime story?
Ygor (*recoiling*) I'll do it for *nowt!*

*He exits up the stairs, keeping well ahead of the Count, who
follows him out*

The Baron puts a hand to his head and paces about the hall

Baron (*with feeling*) What have I got myself into?!

*As he speaks the Phantom sneaks out of the fireplace, pelts him
with a ball of screwed up paper, then retreats*

What the —?! (*Seeing the paper missile*) Who's playing silly buggers?!

The Phantom chuckles loudly off and the Baron shivers. He unfolds the ball of paper and sees what's written on it

(*Loudly, aghast*) This is damnable! *Damnable*!

Ygor, Frau Lurker and the Baroness rush in from DL. *The Baroness still holds a glass, but it's a much larger one*

All What is it? What's wrong?
Baron (*brandishing it*) Another letter!
The Others From *Poo?*
Baron (*coldly*) From P.O.O. Listen...! "Baron, my protégée, Isabel Channing" ——
Ygor (*suddenly*) Isabel? (*Excited*) Is-a-bell! Is-a-bell!
All Shut up!
Baron — "is approaching rapidly and I want you to make her very welcome... "

Organ music plays as the Phantom's voice takes over. Again they all look above and around them

Phantom (*off*) Remember my previous instructions! Do not influence 'er in any way! If you disobey a calamity beyond any adjective will occur!

The organ music fades out

Baron (*exasperated*) This is insane. (*He crumples the note in his fist*)

Isabel bounces down the stairs, now minus her coat

Isabel (*loudly*) Well hi y'all!

They all turn, gape and then rush to make her welcome

Ygor (*delighted*) Miss Channing!
Baroness (*ditto*) Darling!
Frau Lurker (*ditto*) Luvvy!
Baron (*beaming*) Just in time for *sherry*!
Isabel (*bewildered*) Swell.

Ygor goes to pour her a glass. The Baroness links arms with Isabel and escorts her to sit on the sofa

Baroness We hear you're a singer, my dear.
Isabel (*frowning*) Who fed you *that*?
Baron (*wryly*) One of our other... guests.
Isabel (*sharply*) A creepy guy in a cloak an' mask?
Frau Lurker (*dourly*) We haven't *seen* him yet.
Isabel You don't want to! (*Grimacing*) Folks say he's got no *face*!
Baroness But who is he? Your agent?
Isabel *He* thinks he is. But between you an' me the jerk's just a terrorist who ain't got a proper name!
Ygor (*handing her the sherry*) Not even *Poo*?

The Baroness looks for the bottle behind the cushion, realizes it's been taken and gives the Baron a filthy look. He grins

Isabel What? No, handsome — P.O.O.'s an alias. It stands for *Phantom of the Opera*. (*Wryly*) What a poser!

There is a deathly silence

Baron (*swallowing hard*) Wasn't he the chappie who smashed that theatre chandelier on a bunch of Parisians?
Isabel Yep! After they booed yours truly off stage ...
Baroness (*wide-eyed*) But he's a mass-murderer!
Isabel (*emphatically*) An' a one hundred per cent *fruitcake*.

There's an insane laugh from the Phantom, off. Isabel glances nervously at the walls

He made that management hire me, or else. But ——

Phantom (*off*) Sing, ma chérie! Sing for your Maestro!

Isabel (*shouting*) That's the whole problem ... I *can't*! So push off! (*To the others*) You know who he had me billed as? (*Bitterly*) Kiri Te Kanawa!

Ygor (*shaking his head*) What a bummer!

Isabel (*sadly*) I should never have quit the Bluebell Girls.

She sips her sherry as the others exchange glances

Baron (*perplexed*) So what d'you want me to do, Miss Channing?

Isabel Get the Masked Marauder off my back. Can you do that? How about hypnotism? Or a frontal lobotomy?

Baron (*shaking his head*) Time-consuming and unpredictable. There's a much *simpler* solution.

Isabel (*eagerly*) Oh yeah?

Baron Shoot to kill! Ygor — fetch my revolver.

Ygor Yes, Master. (*He gallops* DL *then turns, depicting a two-way journey with his hands*) And if I meet the Phantom on the way?

Frau Lurker (*grimly*) Hide — or waste the bastard!

Ygor goes and Frau Lurker marches out after him

The Baron and Baroness rise

Baron (*to Isabel*) And now, let's show you to your room.

Baroness (*wryly*) It's the Maria Callas Suite.

Isabel (*rising and knocking back her sherry*) Lead on!

They escort Isabel upstairs chatting amiably. Seconds later the Phantom emerges from the fireplace, sniggering malevolently

Phantom The fools! They'll never be able to outwit *me*. I 'ave more tricks up my sleeve than they realize!

He suddenly clutches his sleeve and extracts a mouse which he throws away in disgust

(*Passionately*) And when they 'ear the midnight hour, they will feel the Phantom's *power*. It will turn their blood to ice. I tell you now — it won't be nice!

With an insane laugh and a swirl of his cape he turns to move UR *and collides with the baronial chair*

(*Agonized*) Merde!

Clutching his injured knee and moaning pitifully, he hops UR *as* ——

—— *the* CURTAIN *falls*

SCENE 2

The same. Shortly before midnight

When the CURTAIN *rises the Baroness is alone on stage. She is still holding a half-full glass of gin and is swaying slightly, clearly two and a half sheets to the wind*

As she speaks her husband enters DL *holding a pot plant*

Baroness (*gesturing upstairs*) But Victor, they're odd! They're abnormal.
Baron No more than others, dearest. In fact ——

He suddenly glances down at the plant and addresses it sharply

What was that?! (*A slight pause*) Don't be cheeky!

He slaps the pot as the Baroness stares at him, bemused. Then he addresses her sternly

You'd better make that last. I've found all the others.

Baroness (*petulantly*) I know.

He exits with the plant

(*Making a face after him*) Spoilsport!

Then she smiles smugly and goes to the table C, picks up the vase of flowers and uses that to top up her drink. Thunder rolls and she shivers, then starts singing a deliberately cheerful song. As she does we hear the main door open and close

Isabel and Talbot — now minus his jacket — come in UR, carrying old tennis racquets. Isabel is in a lively mood

Isabel (*cheerfully*) Well, I never served balls by *moonlight* before ...

Talbot smiles sceptically

But that sure was fun. (*Thumping him on the chest*) You're a real nifty player, Harry!
Talbot (*rubbing his chest, grimacing*) Thanks.
Isabel (*to the Baroness*) Just like Sampras!
Baroness (*eyeing Talbot's shorts*) In dress, as well. D'you practise?
Talbot Nah. I grab what fits.

Bemused, the Baroness sits in the baronial chair

Isabel (*to Talbot*) So what's next?

Frau Lurker marches in from DL, carrying a small bowl

Frau Lurker A pretzel!

She thrusts the bowl at Isabel

Isabel (*grimacing*) No thanks. They taste like Bonios. (*She sits on the sofa at the end nearest C*)

Frau Lurker So what? (*Throwing a pretzel into her lap*) You must,
you *will* be made *welcome*!
Isabel (*glaring at her*) Honestly!

*She drops the pretzel on the floor as Frau Lurker advances on
Talbot and thrusts out the bowl*

Frau Lurker Doggy biccy — *ja*?
Talbot (*taking one reluctantly*) Swell.
Frau Lurker (*patting him on the head*) Gut boy!

He glowers at her as she marches up c

*The Countess descends the staircase wearing an evening dress
and diamonds*

Countess (*frowning*) Baroness — where is your husband?
Baroness On his way, I think. (*Gesturing* DR) But there's a
ginormous spider out there, so he may have been held up.

The Countess frowns again and starts to move R

Talbot (*scratching his arms and shoulders*) I hope to God he hasn't.
It's nearly *midnight*.
Baroness (*sipping her drink*) So?

Ygor shambles in DL.

Ygor (*grinning*) Things may get rather *hairy*, Mistress.
Isabel (*staring at him*) Hairy?
Countess He's a werewolf, my dear. (*She gives Talbot an amused
glance and sits* DR)

Isabel stares at him wide-eyed

Isabel You mean you grow long teeth an' stuff?!
Talbot (*grimly*) You bet! An' the stuff's a riot. (*Gesturing*) If I don't
drop 'em, these shorts are history. (*He scratches his backside,
glancing behind him and scowling*)

Baroness (*to Isabel, eagerly*) Oooh! — a Chippendale!
Ygor (*wryly*) An *Airedale*, more like.
Talbot (*gowling*) Smart alec!

He glares at Ygor, then goes to sit on the sofa next to Isabel, who stares at him askance

The Count strides down the stairs

Everyone turns

Count (*grimly*) I am losing patience! The night is calling and I must obey.
Baroness (*nonplussed, staring round*) *I* can't hear anything.
Count That's because mortal ears are unattuned to the subtle sounds of darkness.
Isabel Oh, we *are* superior — aren't we?
Count *We* are. You're only a pleb!
Isabel (*rising*) Want to bet? See here ——!
Countess (*sharply*) This is no time for arguments. We must be calm.

Isabel stares at her, then sits

Count (*to the Countess*) Calm? How can you expect me to be calm, knowing the appetite which overtakes us at the sound of the midnight bell?!
Ygor (*excited*) The bell! The bell!
All Shut up!
Countess (*to the Count*) You could subdue it.
Count (*agonized*) I can't!
Countess That's because you're a greedy pig!
Count (*shocked*) Ilona!
Countess And that look of innocence wouldn't fool a hamster!

The Baroness giggles inanely

Count (*to the Countess*) D'you despise me that much?

Countess (*sharply*) *More!* Now put a sock in it!
Count (*exasperated*) Ach!
Frau Lurker (*thrusting the bowl at him*) Have a nibble!
Count (*snarling*) The only nibble *I* want is *neck!*
Isabel (*grimacing*) Oh, *gross!*
Baroness (*giggling*) Well, we can't help you there.
Count (*icily*) Oh yes you can, Baroness. *Indeed* you can!

He strides towards her and she shrinks into the chair, scared

Countess (*rising, alarmed*) Vlad — no!

The Count is reaching for the Baroness's throat, baring his teeth

The Baron barges into the hall from DR holding a tray with three glasses of red liquid on it

Baron Success! Triumph! (*Seeing their faces*) Hallo, what's going on?
Count (*gutturally*) Nothing.

He backs away from the Baroness, who stares after him wide-eyed, a hand at her throat. The Baron doesn't notice

Baron (*proudly*) Ladies and gentlemen, after some rooting around I think I've distilled the solution to your problems: wolfsbane flowers and dried garlic which, when consumed, will rid you of all your unsociable symptoms, leaving you free to lead a normal life!

There is polite applause from Ygor and Frau Lurker

(*Wryly*) Of course, you may have to suck mints for a day or two.
Talbot (*growling*) Cut the crap and dish up the dose.
Baron (*irritably*) All right, all right! Ygor, pass these to each of our guests.

He hands him the tray and Ygor does as he says, going first to the Countess. The Baron goes to pour a glass of sherry

Isabel (*to Ygor, pointedly*) But skip me, sunshine.
Baron (*speculatively*) It might do something for your charm.
Isabel (*bridling*) Well that's nice! Thanks a bunch!

The Baron returns to c as Ygor hastily passes the last glass to the Count and retreats

Baron (*raising his glass*) My friends — I give you a toast. Happiness and Normality!

The three guests and the Baroness raise their glasses

All Happiness and Normality!

They drink — the guests grimacing — and then the Phantom's voice is heard

Phantom (*off*) Didn't I warn you what would 'appen if you meddled with my plans? Be'old your potion, Baron! It's not the antidote you think!

The Baron rushes to grab Talbot's glass

Talbot (*staring at the Baron*) What's goin' on?!

The Baron sniffs and then sips from the glass, reacting with horror

Phantom (*off*) You fool! You didn't *listen*! So now — let the calamity I foretold *occur*!

The castle clock starts to toll midnight

Ygor (*wildly*) The clock! The clock!
Frau Lurker It's midnight!

Count (*clutching his throat*) What is *happening*?!

Talbot suddenly convulses, clenching and unclenching his hands, then scratches himself furiously

Isabel (*staring at him*) I dunno — but I hope it ain't catchin'!
Talbot (*agonized*) The *change* is comin'... I can *feel* it!

Isabel hastily sits on the sofa arm as he continues to scratch and growl

Countess (*a hand to her brow, perplexed*) But I feel *ill* ...
Count (*malevolently*) And I feel like ... *supper*!
Baroness Oh no!

She staggers out of the chair and takes refuge behind it as the Countess rises quickly and rushes for the stairs

Countess I need the bathroom!
Count (*catching her and holding her*) You need *blood*!
Countess (*breaking free*) The *bathroom*! I'm going to throw up!

  She races upstairs

Baroness (*calling after her, slightly slurred*) Second on the left ...
  Mind the shtep!

As she's speaking Talbot hoists up his sweatshirt to reveal a distinctly hairy stomach

Isabel (*staring at him, wide-eyed*) Oo-er!

Frau Lurker bravely pushes her bowl at the Count

Frau Lurker Go on — force yourself!
Count (*malevolently*) Out of my way — hag!

  The Count pushes her aside and storms out UR

Talbot has now bent over and is clutching the small of his back, his face a mask of discomfort

Talbot (*tortured*) I'm gonna split, too!
Baron (*helplessly*) Feel free.
Talbot (*an agonized snarl*) Aaaagghhrrrr!!

He bounds off the sofa, facing L, and half-crouches, his arms stretched out rigidly, his fingers crooked. And the cause of his discomfort is an enormous taut bulge in the seat of his shorts. The others all gape

Baroness (*wide-eyed*) *That* never happened to Shamprash!

The Phantom laughs madly, off

> *Talbot bounds out DL. There is a terrific ripping sound and he howls with relief*

Ygor (*wide-eyed*) Oh boy!

Suddenly the air is rent by the sound of loud, sinister organ music and everyone jumps

Baron What on earth ... ?!
Baroness (*staring up and staggering*) It's the Phantom!
Isabel (*rising; exasperated*) Doin' his Dr Phibes routine! Honest to God — it's so *hackneyed*! An' *loud*!

She covers her ears and starts running towards the exit DL, then recoils with a shriek

> *Talbot bounds back into view DL. He now sports monstrous claws, and a stiff bushy tail*

Talbot (*malevolently*) Who loves ya, baby?!
Isabel (*screaming*) Aaah! Get away from me, creep! Help!

He starts chasing her round the hall, bounding over the furniture.
Frau Lurker does her best to distract him by throwing him pretzels

Frau Lurker Sit! *Down* boy!
Ygor *(terrified)* Sanctuary! Sanctuary!

He stares around wildly, looking for somewhere to hide as the music
and the chase continue

Baroness *(over the confusion)* Victor — what did he give them?
Baron *(furious)* Glucose, salt and cochineal! *(Shouting up and*
brandishing a fist) Phantom — I don't know how you managed
it, but I'm going to get you for this! D'you hear?!

The Phantom laughs contemptuously, off

Isabel, screaming, hares off upstairs pursued by Talbot, who makes
a lunge at the Baroness as he goes

Terrified, she grabs the vase to defend herself with, but then changes
her mind, throws out the flowers and drains the rest of its contents.
Ygor tries to hide under Frau Lurker's skirt

  (Simultaneously with this) You'd better stay *hidden* — because if
  you don't, my meddlesome freak — the next calamity will be
  yours!

As he stands there, furious, the music and the Phantom's laughter
reach a crescendo, Frau Lurker and Ygor topple and the Baroness
passes out at his feet

The following action is optional. If it isn't used, Scene 2 ends here

The Lights fade to Black-out for a few seconds

  Frau Lurker, Ygor and the Baron exit in the darkness

When the Lights come up again the Baroness is the only one present
— asleep on the sofa

Eerie up-tempo music begins as Isabel creeps downstairs. At the same time the Count enters UR *and approaches her stealthily, arms outstretched. At the last minute she turns, sees him and screams*

The following sequences occur simultaneously:
A) *The Count chases Isabel out* DL. *Talbot chases Ygor and Frau Lurker from* DL, *across the stage and out* UR. *The Phantom sneaks out of the fireplace and exits* DR
B) *The Countess chases the Baron downstairs and out* DL. *Frau Lurker and Ygor, armed with big sticks, chase a yelping Talbot from* UR *across the stage and upstairs. Isabel enters from* DL, *peers about warily and then exits* DR
C) *The Phantom chases Isabel from* DR *across the stage. She goes upstairs, he rushes back into the fireplace. The Count chases the Baron from* DL, *across the stage and out* DR. *Frau Lurker and Ygor rush downstairs and out* DL.

After a moment the Baroness stirs on the sofa. With obvious difficulty she pulls herself up into a sitting position, staring about her in confusion

The Count enters from DR *sees her and licks his lips as he approaches her, arms outstretched. When he reaches the sofa he bends over her with a sinister smile*

At the last minute she looks up — and burps in his face

Again, the following sequences occur simultaneously:
A) *The Count, disgusted, strides out* DL. *Talbot chases Isabel downstairs, across the stage and out* UR. *The Phantom emerges from the fireplace; the Baron, armed with a revolver, enters* DR *and chases him upstairs*
B) *Ygor, brandishing a cross, and Frau Lurker, holding a string of garlic, chase the Count from* DL, *across the stage and out* UR. *The Countess enters warily* DL. *Talbot lopes in* UR, *sees her and chases her out* DR. *Isabel creeps in* UR *and then runs upstairs*

The Baroness burps again

C) *The Count chases Ygor and Frau Lurker from* UR *across the stage and out* DL. *The Countess, armed with a big stick, chases Talbot from* DR *across the stage and upstairs. He yelps fearfully. The Phantom chases Isabel downstairs. As they reach* C *she turns and gives him an almighty slap. He recoils. She exits* DR *as the Baron comes downstairs, still brandishing his revolver. The Phantom sees him, gives a cry of dismay, and disappears into the fireplace. The Baron kicks the side of it angrily and stubs his toe. As he hops about in agony the Baroness turns and waves at him, smiling foolishly. He puts his hands on his hips, looking both incredulous and exasperated as——*

— *the* CURTAIN *falls*

SCENE 3

The same. A few minutes later

When the previous music has ended the CURTAIN *rises to the sound of bats flying and squeaking, then there's a loud wolf howl followed by a scream*

Isabel belts on to the empty stage from DR, *staring off fearfully*

Isabel (*breathless*) Monsters, monsters everywhere — an' not a drop to drink! (*She suddenly notices the sherry decanter*) No, wait! (*Rushing towards it*) There's still some Amontillado!

She quickly fills a glass, takes a mouthful, and then starts singing badly

"I'd love to meet a matador — é *Viva Espana!*"

The Phantom creeps out of the fireplace behind her

Phantom Sing for me! *Sing, ma chérie!*
Isabel (*turning*) What? (*Exasperated*) Oh no — not *you!*
Phantom Oui. Did you think I 'ad gone for good?
Isabel Give me credit! You're tougher to shake off than a virus!
Phantom (*pleading*) But why shake me off? *Why?*
Isabel (*raising her eyes*) Boy, are some guys dense! *Listen.* Not
  only are a lot of your pastimes a real turn-off, but when it comes
  to physical appeal you're distinctly *minus.* Especially in the facial
  department ... That one can politely describe as *zero.*
Phantom But you 'ave never *seen* my face!
Isabel Mister — that's the whole point!
Phantom (*fiercely*) Nor do you want to! The unkind star which 'as
  made me a social nuisance 'as also *deformed* me, making me an
  'ideous freak! Even ma *mum* was scared (*Sadly*) She dumped me,
  'elpless, on an 'ill outside Rouen, to be raised by *'edge 'ogs!*
Isabel (*wryly*) They can't have been choosy.
Phantom They weren't! But then 'edge 'ogs know nothing about
  World War II.
Isabel (*frowning*) What are you talkin' about?
Phantom *Regardez!* Could anything other than an 'edge 'og
  endure *this!*

He removes his mask to reveal a face which is the spitting image of
Hitler. Isabel gasps and recoils

Isabel Aaah!
Phantom This is my secret! What 'ave you to say?
Isabel (*knocking back her sherry, forcibly*) The same as I've said
  all along — *gross, no way* and *Auf Wiedersehen*, pet! I'm off!

She heads for the stairs

Phantom (*pleading*) But Isabel ... !
Isabel (*waving*) Adieu, *Adolf!*

She exits

The Phantom shakes his head sadly

Phantom You will never be my love forever… We will *never* live as one, together.

Another wolf howl is heard, followed by a scream and a yell

    Ygor and Frau Lurker belt in from DL

The Phantom freezes

Frau Lurker (*seeing him and saluting*) Heil Hitler!
Phantom (*disgusted*) Ach!

He turns and goes upstairs

Ygor gapes after him

Ygor I thought he was dead and living in Brazil?
Frau Lurker Rot! He's the landlord of a Bierkellar in Prague.
Ygor Which one?
Frau Lurker *The Jolly Socialist.*
Ygor Ah.

There is another wolf howl and they both cling together

    The Baron creeps nervously in DL

They relax when they see him

Baron (*urgently*) Is the coast clear?
Frau Lurker (*darkly*) For now.
Ygor All the hairy, toothy types are outside.
Baron (*eyeing the fireplace; warily*) What about the Phantom?
Frau Lurker We don't know.
Baron (*scowling*) Blast!
Ygor (*suddenly*) He might be with *Hitler*, Master.
Baron (*staring at him*) What?
Frau Lurker (*elbowing Ygor*) Nonsense! Hitler is *dead*.

Ygor (*confused*) But ... ?
Baron (*irritably*) Of course he is. Now clear off, both of you! And
    if you see any of the guests *distract* them. I need time to make
    another antidote.
Ygor Whatever you say, Master.

Ygor and Frau Lurker start to go

(*Irritably*) What does he expect us to do? Play *Scrabble*?
Frau Lurker (*shaking her head*) Leave that to the rats!

They exit

The Baron paces up and down, frowning

Baron What the hell am I going to do? *Anything* could happen
    between now and dawn! I could be bitten, mauled, clawed or
    deafened by organ works — and *none* of it appeals! (*Suddenly*)
    I'll talk to Elisabeth. She'll know what to do ...

Another wolf howl is heard, then a scream

*The Baroness races downstairs wearing her hat and coat and
carrying a suitcase which is labelled "Duty Free"*

Baroness (*fiercely*) I'm leaving!
Baron Oh fine! Just when I need all the help I can get!
Baroness You've never needed *my* help and you never will — so
    you can cut *that* out.
Baron But where d'you plan on going?
Baroness To Budapest ——
Baron (*drily*) On the wagon?
Baroness (*ignoring him*) — to find people like *me*. Neither
    scientific, sinister nor subnormal — but *nice* people. Human
    beings, in fact! D'you take my point?
Baron Yes — but they won't be easy to come by.
Baroness Why not?
Baron Nice people went out with the Dodo!

Baroness (*heading* UR) So did your common sense! (*Turning*)
Goodbye, Victor.
Baron (*pleading*) Elisabeth!
Baroness May you rest in peace.

She exits

Baron (*angrily*) Damn!

Another wolf howl is heard and he reacts fearfully

Oh hell!

He hurries out DL *as a yell is heard*

*The Phantom races downstairs pursued by Talbot, who now has
a wolfish snout*

Talbot (*savagely*) I'm gonna kill you, you punk!
Phantom (*desperately*) Non! Don't!
Talbot (*snarling and circling him*) Why not?
Phantom Because I didn't know what I was doing — 'oo you were
— what your *problems* are!
Talbot Bull!
Phantom It's true! I'd no idea 'til I saw what 'appened. I only
wanted to mess up the Baron!
Talbot Well you sure messed *me* up. Look at me! The meanest date
in town!
Phantom Well *I'm* no Tom Cruise!

He removes his mask and Talbot recoils

Talbot Cripes! I thought you were dead!
Phantom (*irritably*) I'm not 'itler! I was born like this.
Talbot With the 'tache?

The Phantom nods bitterly

You poor devil!

Phantom Pity accomplishes nothing, Monsieur Talbot. (*Quickly*) But it's nice to 'ear. (*Sighing*) I don't get much else.

Talbot (*drily*) No kiddin'?

Phantom (*sadly*) I'm just as 'aunted and un'appy as you. (*With feeling*) And what I'd give for little succour!

Talbot (*fiercely*) Yeah. Then we could load all *this* on him!

Phantom (*assenting*) Exactement! But as things stand, all we can do is lump it.

Talbot But I don't want to! I wanna be an ordinary guy like I was before. Still goodlookin', mind — but *ordinary*. Not some reject from *Cruft's*!

He lopes UR

Phantom (*following him*) If you *wait*, the Baron might still provide 'ope ...

Talbot (*drily*) You reckon?

Phantom Monsieur — on good days I'm an eternal optimist.

He exits

Talbot stares after him

Talbot (*growling*) With a mug like that, you'd have to be!

He lopes out after the Phantom as bats, flying and squeaking, are heard, then the Countess hurries in from DL, *followed by an exceedingly angry Count*

Count But to pursue a new lifestyle is perverse! You can't hope to find happiness.

Countess Why not?

Count I know from bitter experience.

Countess *Bitter*? Every night for centuries you've been as happy as Larry — chasing mortals for pleasure as much as need!

Count You think *I'm* self-indulgent? What about you and the droves of innocents you lured to *your* castle!

Countess (*defensively*) The world was different then.

Count Yes. Thanks to you it was depopulated!
Countess (*angrily*) At least I learned to moderate my appetite.
Count (*drily*) You didn't learn, Ilona — you *had* to.
Countess Meaning?
Count Everyone under seventy left town!
Countess (*sadly*) True. But that's not the only reason. There has to be more to life than moonlight, malevolence and misery — and I'm determined to find it.
Count (*incredulous*) What you ask's impossible! We're vampires — children of the night — and we can never *change*!
Countess Are you so sure?
Count (*spreading his hands*) Would I be as I am otherwise?
Countess (*drily*) Yes, Vlad, because you're one mean bastard! You can't change because you don't want to. I *do* and I *will*!
Count (*exasperated*) Ach! *Women!*

There is a distant roll of thunder

The Baron backs in from DL, *nervously. Then he turns, sees the others and freezes with his mouth open*

(*Coldly*) Good-morning, Baron.
Baron (*faintly*) Morning? Yes ... I suppose it is.
Count Have you distilled another antidote for us?
Baron (*hesitantly*) No ...

There is a flash of lightning and he jumps

Countess Why not?
Baron I've run out of ingredients.
Count (*menacing*) That's not good enough, my friend. Not good at all!

There is another roll of thunder

The Phantom and Talbot enter UR

The Baron shudders when he sees them

Talbot (*growling*) Just the guy we were lookin' for!
Phantom (*nodding*) Bien sûr!
Baron (*recovering*) Well, how nice that you've found me. (*Grimly*)
Particularly *you*, Phantom. (*He produces his revolver and aims it
at the Phantom*)
Phantom (*reproachfully*) Monsieur! I am your guest.
Baron You're *not*! You're a miserable gate-crasher who's botched
up my plans! And now it's pay-back time!
Countess (*alarmed*) You don't really mean to *kill* him?
Baron Why not? If it hadn't been for him, you'd all be normal!

There is another lightning flash

Phantom (*drily*) Would they?
Baron Of course! D'you doubt my scientific genius?
Phantom Pas du tout. Merely the purgative effect of *Ribena*. For
that was *your* antidote.

The Baron gapes, then looks discomfited

Count (*furious*) Is that true?
Baron (*ashamed*) I'm afraid so.
Countess (*bewildered*) But why?
Talbot (*snarling*) Because he's a failure, that's why!

Thunder rolls again as the Baron retreats from them

Baron (*desperately*) All right, all right — I *am*! And do you know
why? Because I built a laboratory in the back of beyond! Where
there's no electricity, no intelligent man power — God, there isn't
even a Boots to provide me with supplies! D'you blame me for
pretending when my only bits and bobs come from the *grocer's*?!
Count (*fiercely*) Confession comes too late. You must pay the price
for this deception!

The others start moving towards him menacingly

Baron (*recoiling*) No! Stay away from me!

There is a vivid lightning flash

> *Ygor and Frau Lurker rush in from* DL *and Isabel hurries down the stairs*

Ygor (*horrified*) Master!
Isabel (*wide-eyed*) What's happenin'?
Frau Lurker (*with morbid fascination*) They're going to tear him limb from limb!

The others seize the Baron and there's a colossal thunderclap

Baron (*terrified*) Aaah!

> *Before they can do him any damage the Baroness hurries in from* DR *carrying a tray, on top of which are five glasses of liquid*

Baroness (*sharply*) Stop this — *at once!*

Startled, the monsters release the Baron, who's clearly relieved

Baron Elisabeth! You've come back!
Baroness Via the lab. (*To the guests, indicating the glasses on the tray*) Here's your antidote. And there's a glass for all of you.
Isabel All of us?
Baroness (*smiling*) Yes. It will do you the power of good. Believe me.

With varying degress of eagerness they each take a glass

> That's it. (*Cheerfully*) Now — bottom's up!

The guests drink and gradually their faces lighten

Talbot (*wide-eyed*) Somethin's happenin'!
Baroness (*nodding*) I know.
Count (*suddenly*) I don't feel *hungry* anymore.
Countess I don't feel *miserable*.
Isabel I want to sing *Tosca!*
Phantom I want to play jazz!

Talbot suddenly gasps and clutches his stomach

All Save Baroness What's wrong?
Talbot (*fervently*) I want the *john!* (*Quickly*) But it ain't the dose…
    It's those chops I found in the larder. (*Dubious*) I *think* …
    (*Suddenly wide-eyed*) 'Scuse me, folks!

Still with a hand to his stomach, he races upstairs

*The other guests stare at each other and then they, too, clutch their
stomachs as an immense gurgling sound is heard*

Count
Countess ⎫
Isabel ⎬ (*together, wincing*) Ooooh!
Phantom ⎭

Like Talbot, they race out of the hall, using all exits

*The Baroness smiles in satisfaction as Frau Lurker picks up one of
the glasses and stares into it*

Frau Lurker What was *in* these?
Baroness (*itemising on her fingers*) Some fermented All-Bran,
    prune juice, syrup of figs …

The Baron, Ygor and Frau Lurker grimace

    And a week's dose of Ex-Lax.
Ygor (*crossing his legs desperately*) Oooh, Mistress!

Baroness (*smirking*) A simple but effective cure for people with "problems". (*Pointedly*) I thought it was very noble to admit your defects, Victor. *Very.*
Baron (*ruefully*) Yes, but that didn't impress *them*. And they're bound to come back, you know ...

He shivers fearfully

Baroness (*emphatically*) Not straight away.

Ygor and Frau Lurker smirk

And when they do, *we'll* be on Isla Nublar.

Reaching inside her dress she produces a handful of airline tickets and waves them, but the Baron looks strangely worried

Frau Lurker Isla *what* ——?
Baroness (*enthusiastically*) A new tourist resort near Costa Rica.

A look of fearful realization spreads across the Baron's face

(*Oblivious*) Warm, sunny, *exciting...*
Baron (*sharply*) And downright *dangerous*, darling.

The Baroness looks bewildered

It's *Jurassic Park*!

Everyone reacts with horror as the Lights start to dim. We hear the sound of heavy feet pounding the earth, followed by an enormous roar and——

—— *the* CURTAIN *falls*

FURNITURE AND PROPERTY LIST

On stage: Large baronial chair
Old fashioned sofa. *On it* : cushions
Two library chairs
Low table (c). *On it* : vase of flowers and hand-bell
Table (R). *On it* : candelabra
Table (L). *On it* : candelabra
Table (UR). *On it* : sherry decanter and glasses
Stone fireplace. *On mantel* : jars of biological specimens and
the odd skull. *Above it*: Frankenstein crest
Two stone pillars
Old heraldic banners

Off stage: Conical flask containing Minestrone Cup-A-Soup (**Baron**)
Bag containing small bottles of gin (**Baroness**)
Rucksack with label (**Talbot**)
Blood-stained meat cleaver (**Frau Lurker**)
Half-empty gin bottle and half-full glass (**Baroness**)
Meat skewer (**Frau Lurker**)
Full gin bottle and different half-full glass (**Baroness**)
Small suitcase (**Isabel**)
Full gin bottle (**Baron**)
Larger half-full glass (**Baroness**)

Personal: **Baron**: letter
Baroness: jewellery
Phantom: two letters (one screwed into a ball) and mouse
Isabel: bangles and beads

SCENE 2

Strike:	Conical flask and used glasses
Set:	Clean sherry glasses on table UR
	Talbot's tail bulge behind sofa cushion
Off stage:	Pot plant (**Baron**)
	Old tennis racquets (**Talbot** and **Isabel**)
	Bowl of pretzels (**Frau Lurker**)
	Tray with three glasses of red liquid (**Baron**)
	Big sticks (**Frau Lurker**, **Ygor** and **Countess**)
	Revolver (**Baron**)
	Cross (**Ygor**)
	String of garlic (**Frau Lurker**)
Personal:	**Baroness**: half-full glass
	Countess: diamond jewellery

SCENE 3

Off stage:	Suitcase labelled "Duty Free" (**Baroness**)
	Tray with five glasses of liquid (**Baroness**)
Personal:	**Baron**: revolver
	Baroness: four airline tickets

LIGHTING PLOT

Property fittings required: two candelabra

Interior. The same scene throughout

SCENE 1

To open: Candlelight and long shadows

Cue 1	As the CURTAIN rises *Bright flashes of blue and white light off* R	(Page 1)

SCENE 2

To open: Candlelight and long shadows

Cue 2	The **Baroness** passes out *Black-out; then bring up previous lighting*	(Page 31)

SCENE 3

To open: Candlelight and long shadows

Cue 3	**Baron**: "No ..." *Lightning*	(Page 39)
Cue 4	**Baron**: "... you'd all be normal!" *Lightning*	(Page 40)

Cue 5   **Baron**: "Stay away from me!"   (Page 41)
           Lightning

Cue 6   **Baron**: "It's *Jurassic Park!*"   (Page 43)
           Slow fade to black-out

EFFECTS PLOT

Cue 39	**Count**: "Not good at all!' *Thunder rolls*	(Page 39)
Cue 40	**Talbot**: "... that's why!" *Thunder rolls*	(Page 40)
Cue 41	They seize the **Baron** *Colossal thunderclap*	(Page 41)
Cue 42	The guests clutch their stomachs *Immense gurgling*	(Page 42)
Cue 43	The Lights start to dim *Sound of heavy feet pounding the earth, followed* *by an enormous roar*	(Page 43)

COSTUME SUGGESTIONS

Baron: evening wear under laboratory coat.
Baroness: coat over evening dress and jewellery.
Ygor: collarless shirt, scruffy tailcoat which is far too big, scruffy trousers, large shoes, and hump.
Frau Lurker: floor-length black dress. Black leather gloves.
Talbot: denim jacket, light-coloured sweatshirt, knee-length white or "stone" chino shorts, socks and white trainers. (See Make-Up and Special Effects for further details.)
Isabel: coat over 'flapper' dress. Bandeau, bangles and beads.
Phantom: white tie, tails, opera cloak, gloves and mask.
Countess: large hooded cloak over evening dress and diamonds.
Count: much the same as the Phantom, but with a floor-length black cloak.

MAKE-UP AND SPECIAL EFFECTS

Vampires
To create fangs use tooth whitener on the canines and tooth black on the incisors. Use ivory make-up, not white. Line the eyes. Darken the lips.

Phantom
All that matters is the Hitler moustache and the hair slicked over one eye. Make sure the mask covers his moustache.

Ygor
He can be as ugly as you wish. His hair should stand on end and he must look as if he hasn't had a bath in years.

Frau Lurker
Her face should be very severe and her hair should be scraped back into a bun. A faint moustache is very effective.

Talbot
Designer stubble and hairy points to his ears to start with work well. Hairy legs, too, if the actor possesses them! Then, when he leaves the stage after speaking to the Baron, he should enhance/darken his teeth. In Scene 2, when his transformation begins, he first hoists up his sweatshirt to reveal a hairy stomach (fun-fur cummerbund), then wedges a suitably large and sturdy item (which won't fall out!) in the seat of his shorts to create a convincing tail bulge. After loping off stage he *quickly* removes this and dons a pair of "monster hands" (i.e. gloves) as a member of the stage crew attaches a bushy tail to the back of his shorts. It should be convincing, rigid and constructed in such a way that it can be hooked over his waistband without it slipping or falling off, the means of attachment being hidden by his sweatshirt. At the end of Scene 2 the actor has time to affix a wolfish snout before his appearance in Scene 3, and care should be taken that it blends into the rest of his make-up.

N.B. Most of the above items can be made at home if you have the talent and ingenuity. Wolf outfits supplied by costumiers generally evoke the wrong kind of laughter and are to be avoided at all cost!